THIS DOODLE BOOK BELONGS TO

NAME: _Victoria Reti_

DATE: _2019 15 Jan_

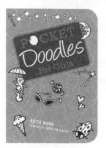

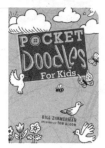

CANADA DOODLES

MEGAN RADFORD
DRAWINGS BY PETER COOK

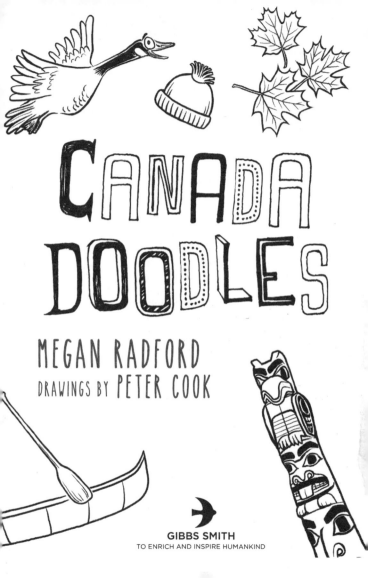

GIBBS SMITH
TO ENRICH AND INSPIRE HUMANKIND

To my family: Sheri, Jaret, and Mum,
who have made every day a crazy adventure.
—M. R.

To Clarence Porter, who taught me that the most
important part of drawing is to have fun!
—P. C.

Manufactured in Altona, Manitoba, Canada
in January 2014 by Friesen

First Edition
18 17 16 15 14   5 4 3 2 1

Published by
Gibbs Smith
P.O. Box 667
Layton, Utah 84041

1.800.835.4993 orders
www.gibbs-smith.com

Cover designed by Michel Vrana; interiors by Virginia Snow
Gibbs Smith books are printed on either recycled, 100%
post-consumer waste, FSC-certified papers or on paper
produced from sustainable PEFC-certified forest/
controlled wood source. Learn more at www.pefc.org.

ISBN: 978-1-4236-3621-2

Want to learn more about Canada?
Come with me, your jolly toothy friend, and
I'll show you all the corners of this country.

Decorate this polar bear's swim trunks
as he dives into the freezing water
for an annual polar bear swim!

Add sprinkles and icing to decorate your tasty Tim Hortons donut.

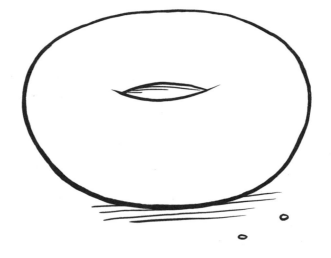

Draw yourself as conductor of a
Canadian Pacific Railway train.

Doodle the train passing through the Rocky Mountains.

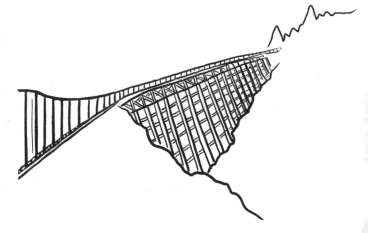

The Group of Seven was famous for
their paintings of Canadian landscapes.
Draw your own landscape masterpiece.

What are your favourite books by Canadians? Who are your favourite Canadian authors?

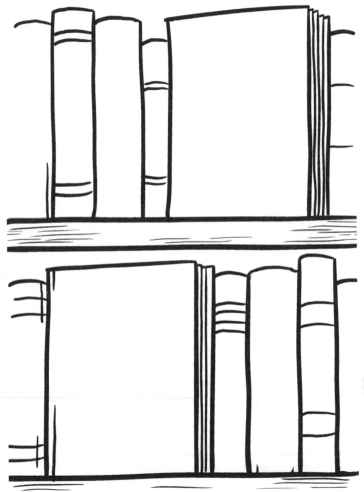

1967 was Canada's 100th-year celebration, and the year of Expo 67, the World's Fair in Montreal. Draw some sparkly party hats, noisemakers, and sunglasses on these fairgoers.

Write a message and draw a picture of Canada for your friend on this postcard.

Draw some aliens as they help
manoeuvre the Canadarm.
What are they trying to attach?

Canada is famous for being REALLY cold. What snug winter gear will you wear to beat the chill? Don't forget your toque to keep your head warm!

Draw two teams of dragons
racing these dragon boats.

Design suits for the hosts of Hockey Night in Canada.

This beaver is taking a wicked
slapshot at the other team's goal.
Did he score, or did the goalie save it?

This poor moose has forgotten the
lyrics to Canada's national anthem!
Help him by filling in as many as you can.

This attractive hockey-playing fella has lost a couple of teeth! Draw his lucky playoff beard and helmet to get him game-ready.

This orca, moose, and grizzly bear
are cheering at a hockey game.
Draw them as they do the wave.

List all of the Canadian NHL hockey teams and your favourite players.

Draw this hockey player giving the
championship trophy a kiss after winning it.
What jersey is he wearing?

Canada has two national sports—
hockey and lacrosse. Draw your
lacrosse stick, helmet, and padding.

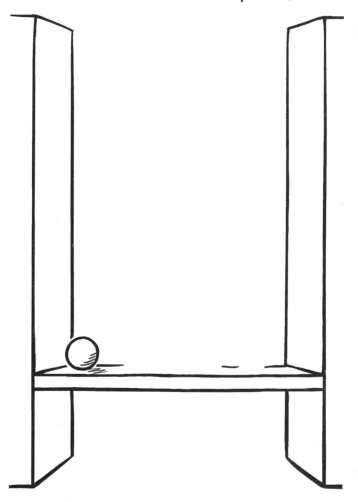

Draw one of each of Canada's coins:
the nickel, dime, quarter, loonie, and toonie.

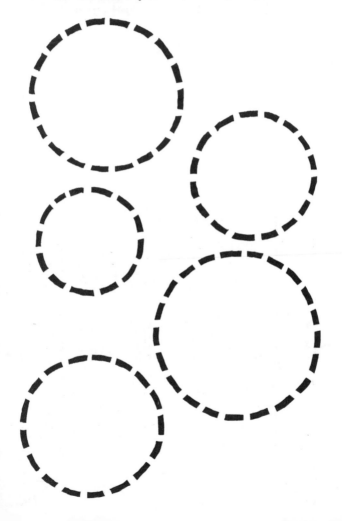

You're rich! Dive into a pool
of loonies and toonies.

Decorate your snowman with the
wackiest materials you can find.

Usually icebergs show only one-ninth of their volume above water. Draw yourself taking a cruise on this iceberg—what does it look like beneath the water?

The Trans-Canada Highway between Victoria, BC, and St. John's, NL, is one of the world's longest national highways, and is often driven end to end. Write a playlist for your long drive.

WEST COAST JAM | **CANADIAN SHIELD MIX**

PRAIRIE PLAYLIST

ATLANTIC TUNES

Draw or write about your favourite
Canadian singers and actors.

The British royal family often pays visits to Canada. Show yourself meeting the queen. (Make sure you wear a suitably fancy hat.)

The two main languages spoken in Canada are English and French. Can you match these English words to their French equivalents?

MAPLE LEAF

CASTOR

SNOW

FEUILLE D'ERABLE

BEAVER

LITTORAL

POLAR BEAR

NEIGE

COASTLINE

OURS BLANC

Draw a bald eagle family in their aerie (nest) at the top of this arbutus tree.

Five-pin bowling was invented in Canada— doodle yourself landing a strike!

Canadians eat more macaroni and cheese than any other nation on earth. Grab a fork and dig in—what toppings are on your mac 'n' cheese?

Santa Claus has his own postal code in Canada: HOH OHO. Write a letter to Santa and be sure to tell him what's on your list this year.

Dear Santa,

SANTA CLAUS
NORTH POLE
HOH OHO
CANADA

The CBC is Canada's national broadcasting service. Now you're at the helm in headphones and microphone. What kind of show are you hosting?

Write a list of guests you'd like to interview.

Finish drawing a neat V of flying Canada geese, honking as they go by.

Draw the geese scattering into a wild goose chase as they go after a group of bugs!

These monarch butterflies are fuelling up on nectar in southern Canada before hitting the road to Mexico. Draw some flowers for them to feed on.

Jump into this pile of maple leaves someone just raked up.

"The Log Driver's Waltz" is a Canadian folk song well known to Canadian children. Draw yourself dancing on a log.

Draw a beaver on his dam watching you go by and dancing along!

Draw this lumberjack's boots,
suspenders, flannel shirt, and hat.

Design a new uniform for the Royal Canadian Mounted Police (RCMP).

Canada boasts two world-class national soccer teams. Doodle a soccer ball running away from being kicked.

Canadians love to eat beaver tails—not the real kind, but the fried pastry variety. Doodle your own tasty version.

This Atlantic cod and this Pacific
salmon are in a kung fu fight!
Draw their fast fins and kicks.

List your favourite animals that can be
found in the Great White North, and
draw a picture of them having a picnic.

Invitation List

Canada has a whole bunch of fabled lake monsters, including Lake Manitoba's Manipogo, Okanagan Lake's Ogopogo, and Lake Champlain's lake monster Champ. What do you think these monsters actually look like? Draw them, scales and all!

Canada has over 30,000 lakes!
Draw yourself some goggles and
flippers and get ready for a swim.

This Canada Post mail carrier is being chased by a dog—show his mail flying through the air!

Design a set of Canada Post stamps.

Canadians developed the McIntosh and Spartan apples, but now this worm wants a bite. Draw him with a knife and fork, getting ready for a feast.

Canadians have a unique way of talking from province to province, eh? Make a list of the distinctly Canadian words you see and hear. Can you define these terms: bunny hug, chinook, chesterfield, Habs, and skookumchuck?

WEST COAST

CANADA'S WEST COAST IS CHOCK
FULL OF BEAUTIFUL RAINFORESTS
AND COASTLINES!
COME ON OVER AND LET'S EXPLORE!

Draw yourself giving a big hug to an old-growth tree in BC's Cathedral Grove.

Draw the rings of this tree.

Draw the tonnes of water dropped by the Martin Mars water bombers on this raging forest fire. The red-and-white planes can scoop up a load of water in about 25 seconds.

Duncan, BC, boasts the
largest hockey stick in the world.
Draw it on the building it calls home.

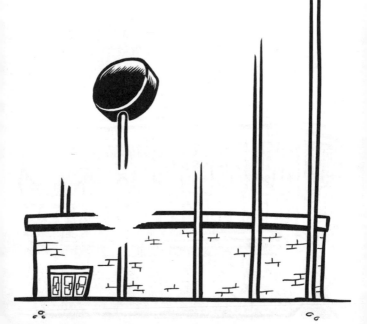

Draw the goats on the roof of the famous Old Country Market in Coombs! What are they eating?

Chow down on a Nanaimo bar in Nanaimo on Vancouver Island. Show your giddy face covered in chocolate.

Nanaimo is home to the annual bathtub festival and race! Get your shower cap on and soup up your tub for the ocean race.

Symphony Splash in Victoria is a symphony performance that takes place on a floating barge in the inner harbour. Draw yourself in a kayak listening to the show.

Famous BC artist Emily Carr was known for
her paintings and her pet monkey Woo.
Draw a fancy outfit for Woo.

This Vancouver Island marmot is having tea and scones at the Empress hotel—what fancy fare is he eating?

Decorate your Volkswagen van before you head to the Gulf Islands off BC's coast. What do your bumper stickers say?

Don your wetsuit before catching some
gnarly waves at Long Beach by Tofino.
Which sea creatures are cheering you on?

Draw a pod of orcas in an awkward family photo.

These fuzzy sea otters want to take a nap.
Draw them holding paws (rafting),
and give them some sea urchin
snacks for when they wake up.

This humpback whale is breaching in the sunshine before migrating down to Baja, Mexico! Draw his splash and give him some summery accessories.

What do these people see from the deck of this BC ferry?

BC is home to the world's largest octopus: the giant Pacific octopus. Draw him as he receives a manicure in a chic Vancouver salon.

Design some rain boots and an umbrella
to keep you dry from Vancouver's rain.

Listen to these buskers (street performers) playing at Granville Island. What are they singing?

Design a fashionable outfit for this pampered pooch in Vancouver's Yaletown district.

The Vancouver Art Gallery is a regular gathering spot for rallies and demonstrations. What are these people protesting? Fill in their signs.

What is this Vancouver street cart selling?

Vancouver is often referred to as "Hollywood North." Draw a Hollywood-esque sign for Vancouver on this hill overlooking the city.

Cherry blossoms fall from the trees during the annual Vancouver Cherry Blossom Festival. Fill these branches with blossoms.

Draw your favourite kinds of sushi.
Don't forget your chopsticks!

Finish drawing this famous totem pole found in Vancouver's Stanley Park.

Run away from the sasquatch at Whistler! Draw your sprinted path down the mountain.

Osoyoos has Canada's only
banana plantation. Make yourself
a tasty banana split.

Draw a group of moose white-water rafting at Hell's Gate rapids.

During the gold rush, the Cariboo region had camels! How many humps does this camel have? Watch out for him spitting at you!

You've struck it rich panning for gold!
Draw your sparkling bounty.

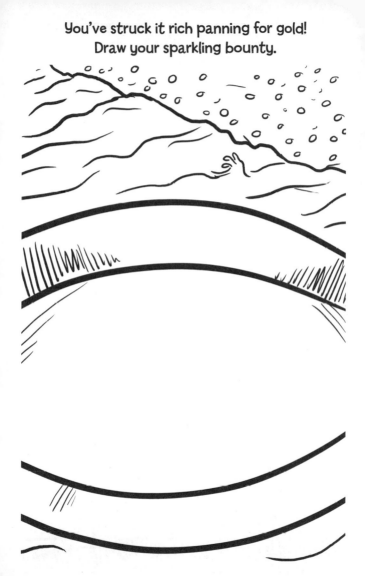

PRAIRIES

THE PRAIRIES ARE A PLACE OF BIG FIELDS AND BIG SKIES. LET'S GO EXPLORE!

Decorate your snowboard before hitting the slopes in Jasper, Alberta.

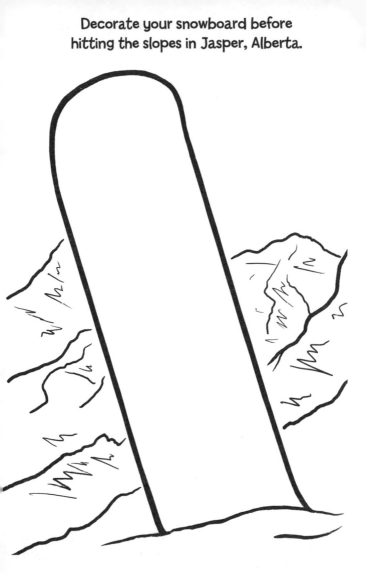

This bighorn sheep has climbed the Rocky Mountains—what can he see from the top?

What's in your backpack for a picnic at Lake Louise? Watch out for that grizzly bear—he's after your snacks.

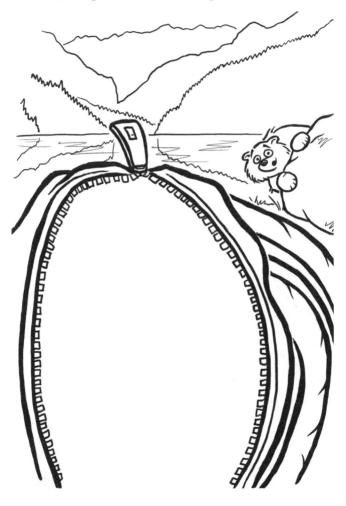

Banff National Park features wildlife overpasses above the highway. Draw a pack of moose driving convertibles across one.

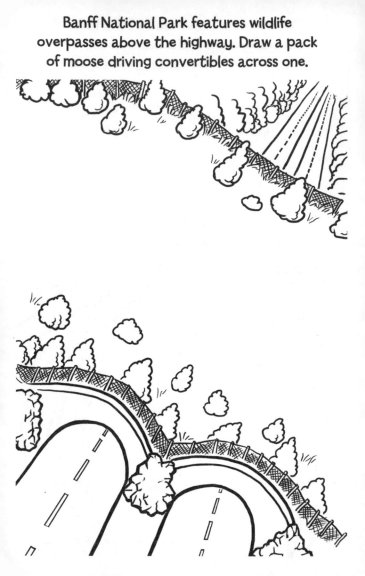

Draw some elk in fancy bathing suits as they take a dip in the Banff hot springs.

Ride the waterslides at the West Edmonton Mall. What are you shouting? Finish drawing the slide.

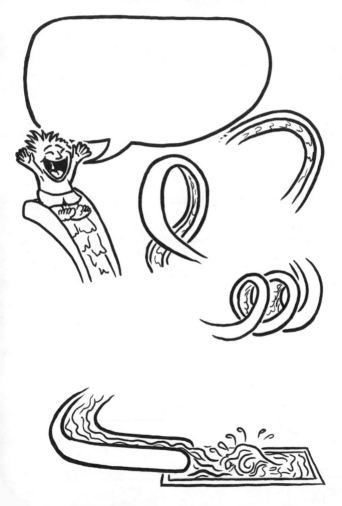

You struck oil! Do a jig to celebrate!

Drumheller is home to the largest dinosaur in the world—a fearsome Tyrannosaurus rex! Draw him brushing his ferocious teeth.

Draw this T-rex doing push-ups to get ready for tourists.

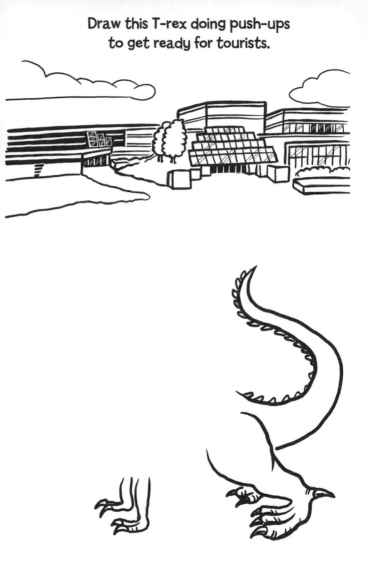

Decorate this cowboy's shirt and boots as he rides a bucking bronco at the Calgary Stampede.

Give this tourist some cowboy
gear from head to toe.

Hold on tight as you take a bobsled ride at Calgary Olympic Park! Draw your scared face.

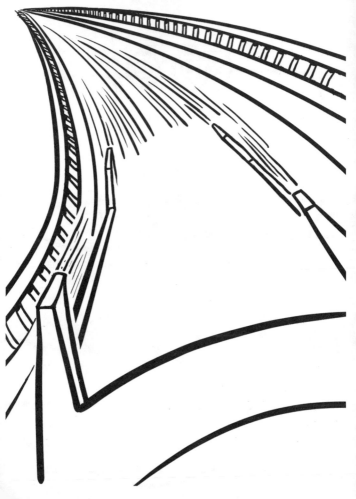

What are these passengers on the CTrain talking about?

Draw helmets on these buffalo to
protect them as they go over
Head-Smashed-In Buffalo Jump.

Draw some pointed ears on the citizens of the town of Vulcan, Alberta.

Hoodoos are tall, thin rock formations pointing skyward in the Alberta badlands. Draw more hoodoos sticking up from this prairie landscape.

Draw an Albertosaurus (a close relative of the later T-rex) and a ceratopsian (horned dinosaur) playing hide and seek in Dinosaur Provincial Park.

Prairie skies go on forever!
What shapes do you see in the clouds?

The town of St. Paul built a UFO landing pad in 1967. Draw a UFO touching down. What sign will you hold up for our intergalactic visitors?

Saskatchewan has a whole bunch of big stuff! Draw a few of the extremely oversized objects that live here:

a coffee pot, woolly mammoth replica, honeybee, and the world's largest tomahawk and red paper clip.

Saskatchewan is the home of universal health care in Canada. Write a get-well-soon message on this man's cast.

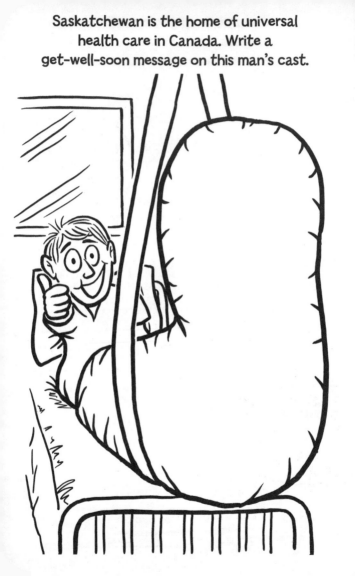

Go through the perogie drive-through
in Saskatoon. What toppings
will you put on yours?

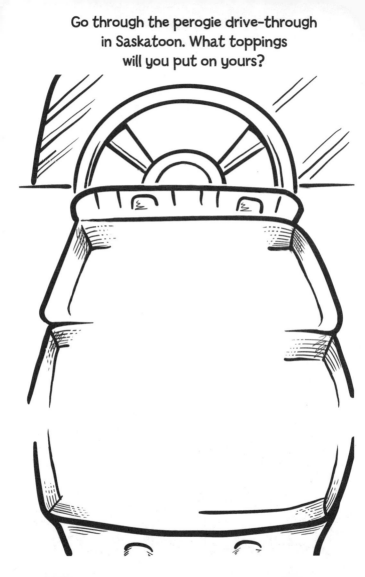

This prairie rattlesnake really
likes saskatoon berries! Draw him
chowing down on a big bowlful.

Draw a fearsome scarecrow to protect your crops.

Can you find your way through this corn maze?

Ride this tractor through a canola field.

Draw the lightning and stormy sky of a prairie storm.

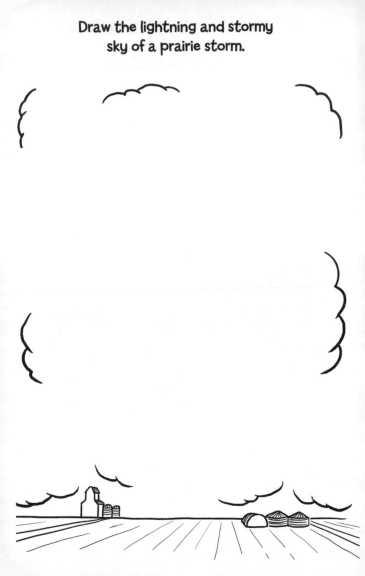

Moose Jaw is the mural capital of North America. Draw your own mural on this back-alley wall.

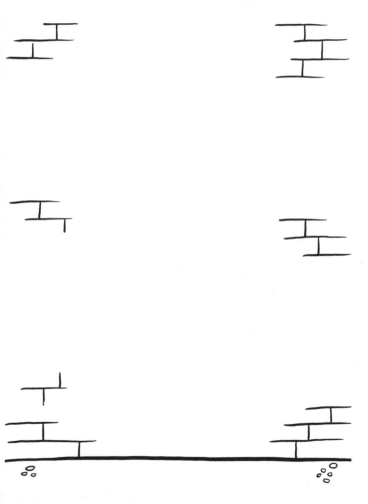

The Big Muddy Badlands in Saskatchewan were once used by outlaws from the American West. What did these outlaws steal?

Who's chasing after them?

Draw a ballerina performing for the Royal Winnipeg Ballet, Canada's oldest dance troupe.

The romance publisher Harlequin started in Manitoba. Design some book covers for your new publishing company.

For more than ten years, Manitoba has been named the Slurpee capital of the world! Draw these people gulping down their cool drinks on a scorching hot day.

Draw more ducks diving for
treats in Assiniboine Park.
Throw them some bread crumbs.

Draw funny faces on these red-sided garter snakes, which annually collect in the Narcisse Snake Dens.

Dodge this ferocious pack of black flies
coming after you! Draw the flies
as a tough motorcycle gang.

Cook yourself some marshmallows over the fire while camping at Grand Beach.

Churchill, Manitoba, is known as
the polar bear capital of the world.
Draw these bears in Winnipeg Jets jerseys,
playing hockey on an outdoor rink.

CENTRAL CANADA

SOME PEOPLE IN CANADA CALL THIS
THE CENTRE OF THE UNIVERSE!
LET'S HAVE A LOOK-SEE AT WHAT'S OUT
OF THIS WORLD ABOUT CENTRAL CANADA.

Draw a herd of Lilliputians tying down
Sibley Peninsula's Sleeping Giant.

A colony of stray cats has long hung out on Parliament Hill in Ottawa, where Parliament votes on potential laws and discusses government action. Draw some cats in Parliament, arguing with one another.

Finish drawing the Peace Tower
in the Centre Block of Ottawa's
Parliament buildings. Decorate it with
some peace signs of your own.

Canada Day fireworks are exploding over
Parliament Hill. Doodle them in the sky.

Draw some figure eights as you skate
on the Rideau Canal, the world's largest
skating rink when the water freezes.

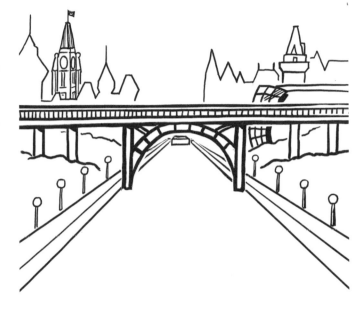

Draw the people you can see on the street below from the top of the CN Tower.

A gorilla is climbing the CN Tower!
Draw him chasing after a banana on top.

What are these tourists on a
double-decker bus taking pictures of?

These two actors are performing in a play at the Stratford Shakespeare Festival. Draw their costumes. What are they saying?

Collingwood, Ontario, has an annual Elvis Festival! Draw some shades and jumpsuits on these excited attendees.

Kingston, Ontario, was the first capital of Canada,
when it was referred to as the United Canadas.
Can you name the current capital cities of
all of Canada's provinces and territories?

1. wighthorse
2. Victoria   8. _____
3. EdMitin   9. _____
4. yellowKiße   10. _____
5. _____ 11. _____
6. _____ 12. _____
7. _____ 13. _____

Fill in these peacocks' stylish
feathers as they strut around
the High Park Zoo in Toronto.

Eat some tasty dumplings in Toronto's Chinatown. What does your fortune cookie say?

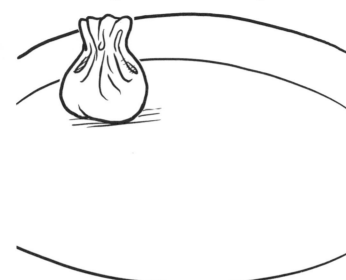

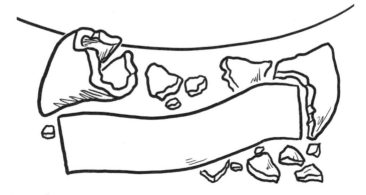

Catch a home run at a Blue Jays game. Which baseball player would you like to sign it?

Your face is on the Jumbotron!
Draw your expression.

Draw the colourful costumes and headdresses at the Caribbean Carnival Parade.

**Finish drawing this streetcar and
ring the bell for your stop.**

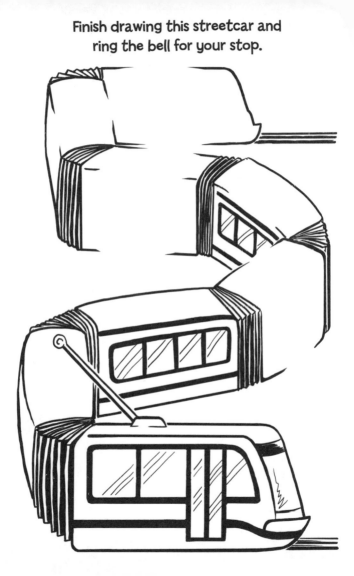

Design the outfits of these fabulous celebrities and the flurry of flashbulbs on the red carpet at the Toronto International Film Festival.

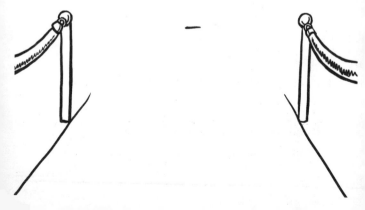

The paparazzi discovered you at TIFF! What do these tabloid headlines say about you?

Draw the planes landing at Pearson International Airport. Where are they arriving from?

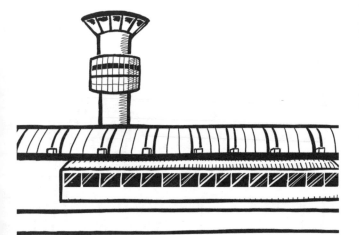

The Toronto Comic Arts Festival is a huge
exhibition for cartoonists and authors alike!
Design your own comic book character to show.

Fill your shopping bag with treats and goodies at the St. Lawrence Market. What did you buy?

This woman is wearing outrageous fashions for Toronto Fashion Week. Draw them!

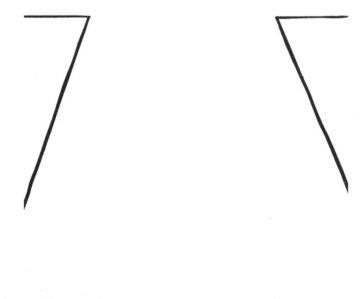

Sophisticated businesspeople on Bay Street are headed to work—draw them lugging their briefcases and talking on cellphones.

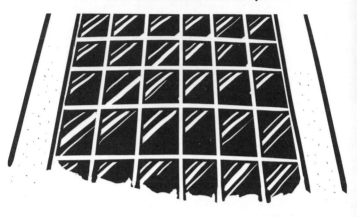

Draw the tops of these skyscrapers on the Toronto skyline.

Doodle some squirrels playing
Frisbee in Trinity Bellwoods Park.

This crowd is dancing in Yonge-Dundas Square. Add some neon signs and draw what's on the big screen.

What do you see from the top of the Ferris wheel at the Canadian National Exhibition?

Create a new ride at the CNE
with lots of loops and whorls!

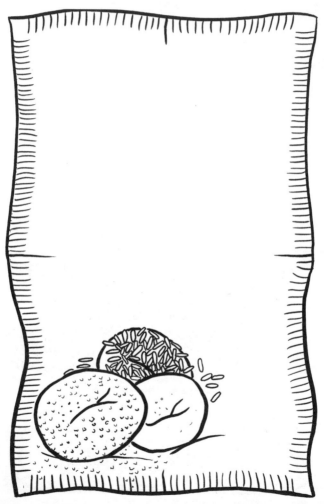

What is this fashionable cyclist on Queen Street wearing?

Decorate these dragons in the
annual Chinese New Year parade
in Toronto's Chinatown.

Decorate yourself with your jersey
of choice and cheer with soccer fans
at this College Street restaurant.

These two knights are jousting at Medieval Times! Draw their suits of armour.

Draw yourself in the stands in medieval garb. Who are you cheering for?

The Art Gallery of Ontario houses more than 80,000 works of art! Create your own masterpiece on this blank canvas. Voila!

Draw a Toronto Raptor making
a wicked slam dunk.

Decorate these fabulous shoes on display at the Bata Shoe Museum.

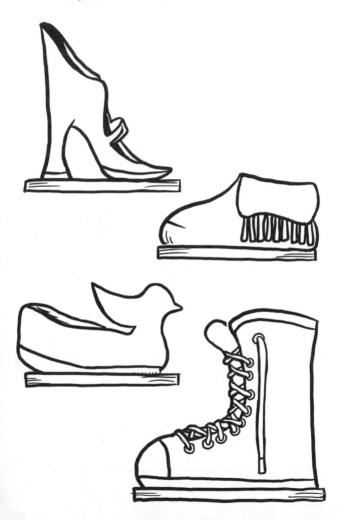

Draw the people and their dogs
waiting for the Toronto subway.

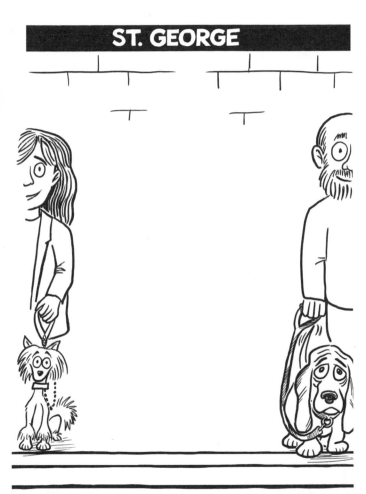

ST. GEORGE

Head on over to Centre Island. Draw some pigeons sunbathing on the beach.

What are these hip Torontonians in Kensington Market wearing?

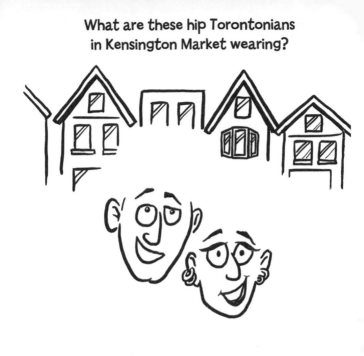

Decorate the turrets of Casa Loma castle.
Create your own flag to fly
from the highest turret.

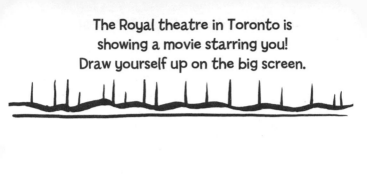

The Royal theatre in Toronto is
showing a movie starring you!
Draw yourself up on the big screen.

Draw the different birds flying around
your head at Bird Kingdom, the world's
largest free-flying indoor aviary.

This woman is going over Niagara Falls in a barrel! Show the crowd watching as the water carries her over the falls.

Put some toppings on your Montreal-
style bagel before you chow down.

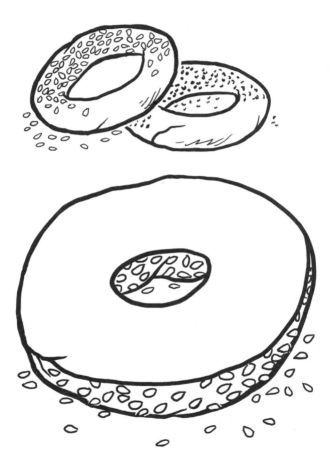

Cirque du Soleil often performs in Montreal, their international headquarters. Draw the striped tent as you enter the show.

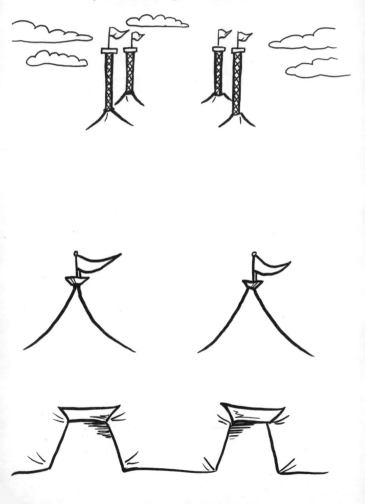

Design costumes for these Cirque du Soleil performers.

These cool cats are grooving at the Festival International de Jazz de Montréal. Draw their instruments.

What is this opera singer singing at the Opéra de Montréal? Draw her costume.

Montreal's subway stops are
famous for their tile patterns.
Design a new pattern for display.

Montreal's Underground City is a huge, interconnecting underground set of tunnels, shops, restaurants, movie theatres, and more. Design a blueprint for your own underground city.

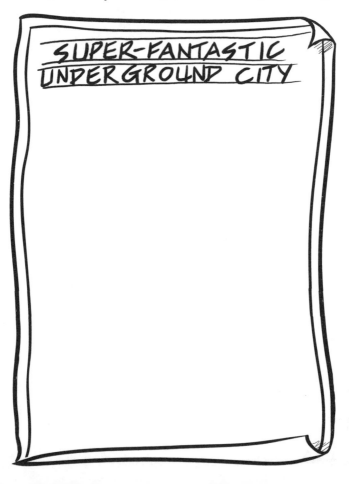

SUPER-FANTASTIC UNDERGROUND CITY

The Montreal Biodome houses replicas of four
distinct ecosystems—draw yourself in each
environment: the Tropical Forest (replica of the
South American rainforest), the Laurentian Maple

Forest (replica of the North American wilderness), the Gulf of St. Lawrence (replica of the local marine life), and the Sub-Polar Regions (replicas of the Labrador Coast and Sub-Antarctic Islands).

What excellent items did you buy at the
vintage shops of Boulevard Saint-Laurent?
Draw your new finds.

Decorate your canoe as you and this
beaver paddle up the St. Lawrence River.

What do you see as you look out from
the Mont Mégantic observatory?
Is that a UFO?!

You discovered a new constellation! Draw and connect some dots and stars to form the constellation, then give it a name.

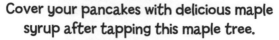

Cover your pancakes with delicious maple syrup after tapping this maple tree.

In the winter, Quebec City is home
to Hôtel de Glace, an ice hotel.
Draw designs on the walls of your icy room.

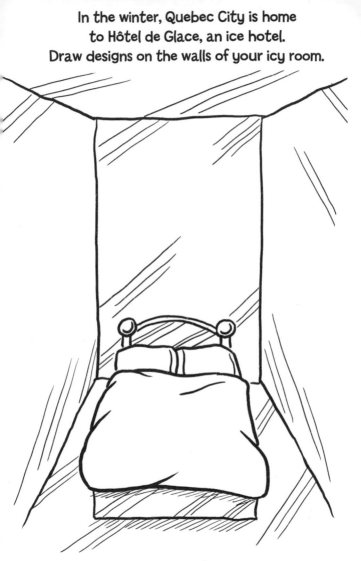

Design and carve your own ice sculpture at the Winter Carnival.

Cover these fries with cheese curds and gravy to make your own oh-so-tasty poutine.

Doodle some beluga whales at
the Saguenay Fjord chasing
after this school of fish.

ATLANTIC CANADA

THE EAST COAST OF CANADA IS ONE OF THE MOST BEAUTIFUL PLACES IN THE COUNTRY, WITH A RICH HISTORY BY THE SEA. LET'S CHECK IT OUT!

Draw the sails of Nova Scotia's Bluenose, Canada's famous fishing and racing schooner.

Oak Island has been the site of lots of treasure hunting over the last few hundred years! Draw yourself striking treasure—what did you find?

Draw a group of porpoises jumping around this fishing boat.

Draw pirate ghosts in this ship sailing around the Halifax Harbour.

Sambro Island has North America's oldest operating lighthouse. Doodle some ships in the harbour saved by its light.

Draw a seal sitting down in a bib for
a nice feast at this seafood buffet.

One million immigrants arrived in Canada through Pier 21. Draw a new arrival and show her reaction to being in a new country.

These fiddlers are playing a jaunty tune!
Draw their fiddles. What are they singing?

Draw these bagpipers' kilts and bagpipes at the Antigonish Highland Games.

The Bay of Fundy has the highest tidal range in the world. Draw all the creatures basking on the sand at low tide.

Draw a few Bay of Fundy sea monsters having a dance party in the harbour.

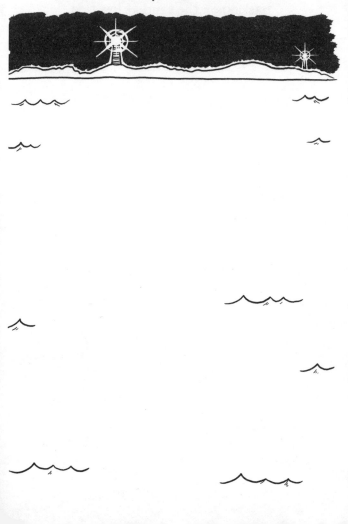

Try to reel in a big Atlantic salmon.
What did you catch?

Build your own sandcastle at the annual New River Beach Sand Sculpture Competition.

New Brunswick has its very own Chocolate Museum. Draw all the things you'd like to dip in this chocolate fountain.

The Hartland Covered Bridge is the longest covered bridge in the world, and is also called a kissing bridge. Who mistook this raccoon for his sweetie pie and went in for a smooch?

The small town of Florenceville-Bristol is the home of the McCain empire, which makes one-third of the world's French fries. Draw a towering stack of fries stretching into the sky!

Town of
Florenceville Bristol
"French Fry Capital of the World"

Confederation Bridge links Prince Edward Island to New Brunswick. Draw a superhero coming in to rescue a bear in distress on the bridge support.

Anne of Green Gables is PEI's most
famous spunky redhead.
Draw Anne's braided hair and freckles.

Draw windmills spinning in the wind currents at the Wind Energy Institute of Canada in PEI.

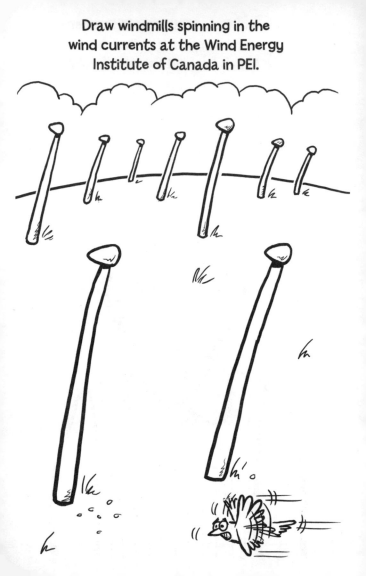

Dig for clams off the coast. Doodle a superclam made of little ones as they battle back against the digger!

It's a windy day on the coast.
Design a kite and take it for a spin.

PEI has over thirty golf courses!
Draw some fancy golf duds for yourself
as you chip from a sand trap.

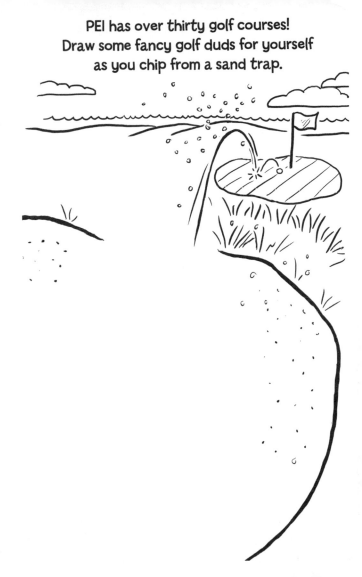

This mermaid is trying to catch this fisherman's attention. Give her some flowing hair and starfish attire.

This colony of Atlantic puffins is chatting in their Newfoundland accents. What are they saying?

Draw a lobster pinching the bottom of the fisherman trying to catch him!

Give these crabs some clever disguises
to hide from the crab traps!

Draw a group of black bears snowshoeing in Gros Morne National Park.

Newfoundland's Great Northern Peninsula is home to L'Anse aux Meadows, a Viking site. Draw these Vikings' beards as they chomp turkey legs.

ARCTIC

BRRRRR! BUNDLE UP, AND LET'S HEAD TO THE ARCTIC. THERE'S LOTS TO SEE AND DO IN THE LAND OF THE MIDNIGHT SUN.

Finish building your igloo and have
iced tea with a friendly narwhal.

You've reached the top during a rock climbing expedition on Baffin Island. Draw your expression as you base jump down!

This coast guard ship is breaking
apart thick ice in Hudson Bay.
Draw the ice cracking all around it.

Draw running sneakers on these polar bears
as they do some stretches to get ready
for the Northwest Passage Marathon.

During the summer solstice, Nunavut is the land of the midnight sun, with twenty-four hours of sunlight. Doodle yourself going to sleep in the daytime.

The Northwest Territories has Canada's only bear-shaped licence plates. Design your own vanity plate. What does it say?

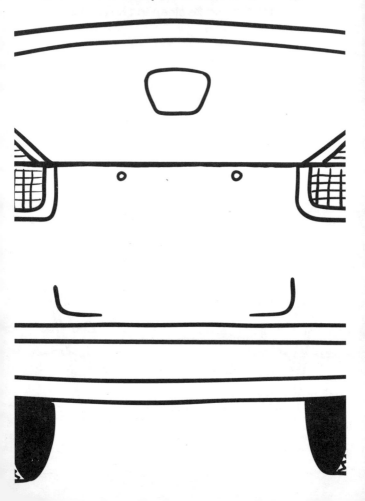

The Grolar bear is a hybrid grizzly/polar bear that was found in the Northwest Territories in 2006. Draw music notes floating through the air as these two bears dance.

Draw what you see in the swirling patterns
of the northern lights (aurora borealis).

Yellowknife is called the Diamond Capital of North America. Draw some fabulous baubles on these mountain goats as they lounge around on their rocks.

This caribou just made an excellent throw in a curling match. Show the other caribou sweepers guiding the rock.

Decorate these signs in Watson Lake's Sign Post Forest.

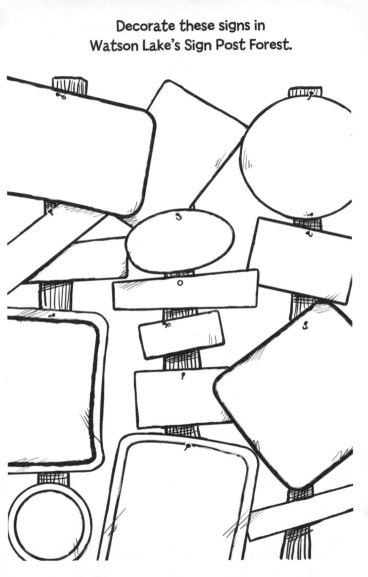

The Carcross Desert in the Yukon
is the world's tiniest desert.
What do you see in this desert mirage?

You're on a zip-lining tour in the Yukon.
What did you catch these grizzly bears doing?

The Yukon Quest is one of the toughest dogsled races in the world. Draw some eager canines pulling your sled.

You've reached the top of Mount Logan, Canada's highest mountain. What do you want to shout from the peak?

Finish this inukshuk, a stone figure resembling a human and built by the Inuit.